Discovering
South
America

SOUTH AMERICA
FACTS & FIGURES

Flags of South America

Argentina   Bolivia   Brazil   Chile

Colombia   Ecuador   Guyana   Paraguay

Peru   Suriname   Uruguay   Venezuela

Discovering South America

SOUTH AMERICA
FACTS & FIGURES

Roger E. Hernández

Mason Crest Publishers
Philadelphia

Produced by OTTN Publishing, Stockton, N.J.

Mason Crest Publishers
370 Reed Road
Broomall, PA 19008
www.masoncrest.com

First printing

1 3 5 7 9 8 6 4 2

Library of Congress Cataloging-in-Publication Data

Hernández, Roger E.
  South America: facts and figures / Roger E. Hernández.
      p. cm. — (Discovering South America)
  Includes bibliographical references and index.
  ISBN 1-59084-299-5
  1. South America—Juvenile literature. I. Title. II. Series.
  F2208.5 .H47 2003
  980—dc21
                                                                    2002011901

Argentina		Paraguay
Bolivia	**South America:**	Peru
Brazil	Facts & Figures	Suriname
Chile	**Ecuador**	Uruguay
Colombia	**Guyana**	Venezuela

Table of Contents

Introduction   **6**
James D. Henderson

The Land   **9**

History   **17**

The Economy   **27**

The People   **35**

The Cities   **43**

A Calendar of South American Festivals   **48**

Recipes   **50**

Glossary   **52**

Project and Report Ideas   **54**

The Countries of South America: Maps   **55**

Chronology   **58**

Further Reading/Internet Resources   **60**

For More Information   **61**

Index   **62**

Discovering South America

James D. Henderson

South America is a cornucopia of natural resources, a treasure house of ecological variety. It is also a continent of striking human diversity and geographic extremes. Yet in spite of that, most South Americans share a set of cultural similarities. Most of the continent's inhabitants are properly termed "Latin" Americans. This means that they speak a Romance language (one closely related to Latin), particularly Spanish or Portuguese. It means, too, that most practice Roman Catholicism and share the Mediterranean cultural patterns brought by the Spanish and Portuguese who settled the continent over five centuries ago.

Still, it is never hard to spot departures from these cultural norms. Bolivia, Peru, and Ecuador, for example, have significant Indian populations who speak their own languages and follow their own customs. In Paraguay the main Indian language, Guaraní, is accepted as official along with Spanish. Nor are all South Americans Catholics. Today Protestantism is making steady gains, while in Brazil many citizens practice African religions right along with Catholicism and Protestantism.

South America is a lightly populated continent, having just 6 percent of the world's people. It is also the world's most tropical continent, for a larger percentage of its land falls between the tropics of Cancer and Capricorn than is the case with any other continent. The world's driest desert is there, the Atacama in northern Chile, where no one has ever seen a drop of rain fall. And the world's wettest place is there too, the Chocó region of Colombia, along that country's border with Panama. There it rains almost every day. South America also has some of the world's highest mountains, the Andes,

Snowy peaks rise over Ushuaia, Argentina, the southernmost city in the world.

and its greatest river, the Amazon.

So welcome to South America! Through this colorfully illustrated series of books you will travel through 12 countries, from giant Brazil to small Suriname. On your way you will learn about the geography, the history, the economy, and the people of each one. Geared to the needs of teachers and students, each volume contains book and web sources for further study, a chronology, project and report ideas, and even recipes of tasty and easy-to-prepare dishes popular in the countries studied. Each volume describes the country's national holidays and the cities and towns where they are held. And each book is indexed.

You are embarking on a voyage of discovery that will take you to lands not so far away, but as interesting and exotic as any in the world.

The geography and climate of South America vary greatly. (Opposite) The massive Perito Moreno Glacier in Los Glaciares National Park, on the southwestern edge of Patagonia. (Right) Iguazú Falls, located at the point where Argentina, Brazil, and Paraguay meet, is made up of about 275 different cataracts that stretch over more than 2 miles (3.2 km).

1 The Land

SOUTH AMERICA IS the fourth largest of the world's seven continents, with an area of nearly 7 million square miles (almost 18 million square kilometers). Measuring from north to south it is the longest continent, stretching 4,600 miles (7,403 km). Its northern tip, La Guajira Peninsula in Colombia, is located about 600 miles (966 km) above the equator. The southernmost point at Chile's Cape Horn is less than 400 miles (644 km) from *Antarctica*. No other continent is closer to the South Pole.

Geographically, South America can be divided into several distinct regions, including mountains, grassy plains, marshlands, and river basins.

The Andes, which run almost the entire length of the continent near the western coast, are second only to the Himalayas as the world's tallest mountain chain. Several peaks rise over 20,000 feet (6,100 meters). The altiplano, a high *tableland* at the heart of the Andes, is dry and bare. Another formation, much lower and much more forested, is the Guiana Highlands in the northeast of the continent, which rise to 9,000 feet (2,745 meters). There are also short mountain ranges in southern Brazil.

As famous as the Andes is the lush Amazon River basin, which has more than 2 million square miles (over 5 million sq km) of water drained by the Amazon River and its more than 1,000 tributaries. The Amazon River itself is 3,900 miles (6,276 km) in length, second only to the Nile, but its volume of water is by far the largest. Almost one-fifth of all the flowing water in the world is carried by the Amazon.

Another important drainage system includes the Paraná, Paraguay, and Uruguay Rivers complex, which empties out into the broad Río de la Plata, an estuary on the Atlantic coast that separates Argentina and Uruguay. Other large rivers include the São Francisco in Brazil, which stretches approximately 1,800 miles (2,897 km), and the Orinoco in Venezuela, 1,340 miles (2,156 km) in length; Angel Falls, the world's highest waterfall at 3,230 feet (985 meters), is also located here.

There are not many lakes in South America. The largest is Lake Titicaca, on the Peru-Bolivia border. At 3,141 square miles (8,132 sq km), it is only the 19th largest in the world, but it lies at an altitude of 12,500 feet (3,812 meters), making it the world's highest. There is also Lago de Maracaibo, in Venezuela; although it is called a lake, its narrow opening to the Caribbean Sea technically makes it a gulf.

The continent's flatlands include the Brazilian plateau, which takes up much of that country south of the Amazon. Another plain extends from the grassy Argentinean Pampas (plains) south into rocky Patagonia. A third, smaller plain is the Venezuelan llanos, squeezed between the Andes, the Guiana Highlands, and the Atlantic Ocean. In the northern half of South America, a strip of flatlands runs along the Pacific coast west of the Andes.

South America also has important wetlands. The Pantanal, in Brazil, is the world's most extensive swamp. Other marshy areas are along the river deltas, especially at the mouths of the Orinoco and the Amazon. Much of the land along those rivers is prone to flooding.

One of the lesser-known geographic features of South America is the coast of southern Chile, with its thousands of islands and islets, *fjords*, and *glaciers* that seem as if they belong not in South America but in Scandinavia.

Climate

The bulk of South America lies between the equator and the *tropic of Capricorn*, and so most of the continent has a tropical climate. But there are notable exceptions. The *Southern Cone* has a temperate climate, and there are bitterly cold regions as well, even in the tropical areas.

The temperate zone is centered on the Southern Cone. Winters are mild and summers are warm but not hot. On the Atlantic side around Buenos Aires, temperatures average 77°F (25°C) in the summer and 50°F (10°C) in the winter; Santiago de Chile on the Pacific coast is a bit cooler.

Regions with hot and humid tropical climates include the rain forests along the Orinoco and Amazon River basins. Seaside cities on the Caribbean and Atlantic such as Caracas and Rio de Janeiro have tropical climates too, as does much of the northern Pacific coast. Temperatures average about 85°F

(30°C), with little seasonal variation and heavy rainfall most of the year.

But not all regions near the equator share a rainy climate. Northeastern Brazil is hot but parched, and the Atacama Desert of northern Chile, near the tropic of Capricorn, is one of the world's driest, with average yearly rainfall of 0.03 inches (0.08 centimeters).

But with altitude as a factor the weather can be blustery in this tropical zone. Temperatures in mountain cities like Bogotá average between 48°F and 68°F (9°C and 20°C), depending on the season. In the high Andes it can dip below freezing, even near the equator.

The coldest region is the far south. The climate around Tierra del Fuego and surrounding islands is subantarctic, with high winds and average low temperatures below freezing in the winter, rising to only about 50°F (10°C) in the summer.

Flora and Fauna

The tropical rain forests along the Orinoco and Amazon River basins are the world's largest, and the richest as well. In a study conducted in the Brazilian Amazon, near Manaus, scientists found 1,652 different plants of 107 species in an area of only 1,900 square feet (177 square meters)—a small example of the great *biodiversity* of the Amazon, home to as many as 50,000 plant species. These range from the tiniest mushrooms to exotic orchids to the trees of the forest *canopy,* which reach 300 feet (92 meters) tall.

Animal life is amazingly diverse, too. By some estimates there are 30 million insect species—4,000 different kinds of butterflies alone live in the Amazon. Vertebrate life is also rich. Almost one-third of all the bird species in

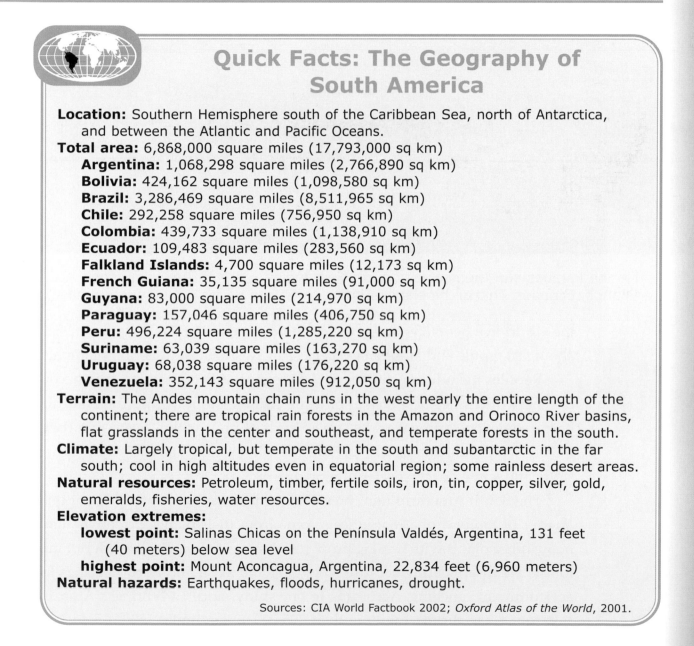

Quick Facts: The Geography of South America

Location: Southern Hemisphere south of the Caribbean Sea, north of Antarctica, and between the Atlantic and Pacific Oceans.

Total area: 6,868,000 square miles (17,793,000 sq km)
Argentina: 1,068,298 square miles (2,766,890 sq km)
Bolivia: 424,162 square miles (1,098,580 sq km)
Brazil: 3,286,469 square miles (8,511,965 sq km)
Chile: 292,258 square miles (756,950 sq km)
Colombia: 439,733 square miles (1,138,910 sq km)
Ecuador: 109,483 square miles (283,560 sq km)
Falkland Islands: 4,700 square miles (12,173 sq km)
French Guiana: 35,135 square miles (91,000 sq km)
Guyana: 83,000 square miles (214,970 sq km)
Paraguay: 157,046 square miles (406,750 sq km)
Peru: 496,224 square miles (1,285,220 sq km)
Suriname: 63,039 square miles (163,270 sq km)
Uruguay: 68,038 square miles (176,220 sq km)
Venezuela: 352,143 square miles (912,050 sq km)

Terrain: The Andes mountain chain runs in the west nearly the entire length of the continent; there are tropical rain forests in the Amazon and Orinoco River basins, flat grasslands in the center and southeast, and temperate forests in the south.

Climate: Largely tropical, but temperate in the south and subantarctic in the far south; cool in high altitudes even in equatorial region; some rainless desert areas.

Natural resources: Petroleum, timber, fertile soils, iron, tin, copper, silver, gold, emeralds, fisheries, water resources.

Elevation extremes:
lowest point: Salinas Chicas on the Península Valdés, Argentina, 131 feet (40 meters) below sea level
highest point: Mount Aconcagua, Argentina, 22,834 feet (6,960 meters)

Natural hazards: Earthquakes, floods, hurricanes, drought.

Sources: CIA World Factbook 2002; *Oxford Atlas of the World*, 2001.

Marine iguanas sun themselves on Isla Fernandina, part of the Galápagos Islands, Ecuador. This archipelago is home to a wide variety of unique animals.

the world live here (85 percent are *endemic*), as do over 2,000 species of fish, about 600 reptile and amphibian species, and a similar number of mammals.

Reptiles include various species of the crocodile family and the anaconda, the world's heaviest snake. Bird life includes toucans, parrots, and the harpy eagle, one of the world's largest birds of prey, with a seven-foot (two-meter) wingspan. Mammals include the pink freshwater dolphin, jaguar, sloth, and some dozen species of monkeys.

The South American rain forests have medicinal value, too. About one-quarter of modern pharmaceuticals come from their plants. Scientists think many other plants with healing properties have yet to be discovered. But rain forests are disappearing because of logging and slash-and-burn clearings for agriculture or ranching. According to one study, since 1978 Brazil's Amazon rain forest has shrunk by more than 205,000 square miles (530,745 sq km), more than 10 percent of its original size. Environmentalists are working to stop *deforestation* in the Amazon, the Orinoco, and along the strip of Atlantic forest on Brazil's southern coast.

Another well-known South American *ecosystem* is the Andes. It is home to the Andean condor, the bird with the largest wingspan in the world. An interesting mammal of the Andean foothills is the spectacled bear; it is the continent's only *ursine* animal, and can weigh up to 500 pounds (186.5 kilograms). Overall, however, the Andes have scanty vegetation and little animal diversity. Only animals adapted to the harsh and cold environment live in the higher altitudes. These include the camel-like guanaco and vicuña and rodents such as the guinea pig.

In the southern part of South America is yet another ecosystem, the Pampas, a large flat plain covered mostly with grasses. Bird life includes the ostrich-like rhea; mammals include the maned wolf; the world's biggest rodent, the capybara; and the cavy, another rodent species.

North of the Pampas is the Pantanal, earth's largest swamp at 55,000 square miles (142,395 sq km). Bird life is particularly rich, with an abundance of wading birds such as egrets, storks, and ibises. Mammals include endemic South American species such as the marsh deer and giant anteater.

Perhaps the least known of South American ecosystem is the temperate forest of southern Chile, which ranges from *deciduous* to *coniferous*. Among the rare animals here are the kodkod, a species of small wildcat, and its large relative the cougar. Farther south at the continental tip, in a rocky and windswept habitat, live cold-weather animals such as killer whales, albatrosses, elephant seals, and penguins.

(Right) South America has been inhabited for thousands of years, but it was relatively recently that Polynesians landed on Easter Island, off the coast of Chile, and carved these strange figures (called *moai*). (Opposite) A statue of Simón Bolívar (1783–1830). One of the great leaders of South America's history, Bolívar freed much of the continent from Spanish control.

2 History

EVIDENCE OF HUMAN settlement in South America dates to at least 10,000 B.C. The original South Americans may have been the descendants of **nomadic** peoples who crossed the Bering Strait into Alaska during the last ice age and slowly made their way south.

Some people ended up in the rain forests, where they continued their nomadic existence well into modern times. Others settled along the coastal plains next to the Andes. By 4500 B.C., they had established farming communities. Eventually, they developed into advanced civilizations.

Indigenous Civilizations

By 2000 B.C., the cultures along the coastal plains and in the Andean foothills had evolved enough to build monumental structures. As the centuries passed, the Nazca, Chavín, and Tiahuanaco people were among those that dominated the region.

They were a prelude to the Incas, the most advanced of the pre-Columbian Andean cultures. The Inca Empire reached its height in the 15th century A.D. The Inca emperor, considered a god, ruled a population variously estimated at between 6 and 12 million people. They lived in a region of some 2,500 square miles (6,472 sq km), extending from a slice of southern Colombia to northern Chile and from the Pacific coast to the Andes.

The Incas were magnificent architects who cut and fit together stone blocks without mortar to build imposing temples. These structures can still be seen in Cuzco and Machu Picchu, in Peru. An extensive road network linked the empire's cities. The Incas spoke the Quechua language, still used by more than 12 million people in Peru, Bolivia, and Ecuador. They did not have an alphabet, but kept records with the quipu, a complex device made of knotted cotton cords that have different lengths and colors.

Conquest and Colonization

As the Incas neared the height of their power, Christopher Columbus landed on the continent of South America during his third voyage, in 1498. Explorations by competing Spanish and Portuguese navigators followed. Their disputes were settled by the Treaty of Tordesillas, in which both sides agreed that everything west of a line at approximately 50 degrees west longitude would belong to Spain, and everything east to Portugal. The treaty accounts for the division of South America into Spanish- and Portuguese-speaking nations.

The ruins of the Inca city of Machu Picchu, high in the Andes Mountains of Peru. The Incas ruled an enormous empire in northwestern South America until the arrival of Spanish conquistadors in the 16th century. In 1533 Francisco Pizarro (inset) led a small army to the city of Cajamarca, where he captured Emperor Atahuallpa and took control of the empire for Spain.

The conquest of South America began in 1532, when Francisco Pizarro landed with fewer than 200 men on the coast of what is now Peru. The Incas had just been through a civil war that severely weakened the empire. Emperor Atahuallpa and some 3,000 of his soldiers met the Spaniards in the city of Cajamarca, where Pizarro demanded that the Inca leader accept Christianity and acknowledge Spain's king, Charles V, as his sovereign. When Atahuallpa refused, Pizarro ordered his strategically placed cannons to open fire.

The Inca soldiers who were not killed in the barrage fled in horror from weapons they had never imagined existed. Atahuallpa was taken prisoner and later executed. Within a year, Spain controlled the Inca Empire.

Spaniards and Portuguese continued to settle the rest of the continent. Pedro Álvares Cabral had claimed Brazil for Portugal as early as 1500, Pedro de Mendoza founded Buenos Aires in 1536, Pedro de Valdivia founded Santiago in 1541, and Diego de Losada founded Caracas in 1567. Lima, the seat of the Spanish viceroyalty that ruled colonial South America for centuries, was founded in 1535.

Spain and Portugal imposed their rule over all South America except the Guianas region between Venezuela and Brazil in the northeast, which was divided among the Dutch, French, and English. Throughout the continent, Indians were killed or forced to hide in the interior. Others mingled with their conquerors, marking the birth of modern-day *mestizo* South American societies. The European colonists also brought African slaves to work the farms and the silver and gold mines that brought great wealth in the 16th century. As years passed, the culture of the Africans also mingled with that of their masters.

In Spanish America, a *hierarchy* grew in which native-born Spaniards occupied the first rank, their South American–born white descendants—called *criollos*—occupied the second, and mestizos the third, followed by the masses of blacks and unassimilated Indians, who lived in extreme poverty and had almost no political rights.

Independence

South Americans began to resent the political arrangements that favored native-born Spaniards. Even the criollos began to see themselves as a people separate from the European-born Spanish and Portuguese. So when a French army under Napoleon invaded Spain in 1808, criollos began to demand the right of self-rule.

Patriots declared *autonomous* governments in several cities. When Spain refused to recognize them, wars broke out. The South Americans were inspired by the American Revolution and its successful effort to overthrow colonial Great Britain.

The leader of South American independence in the south was José de San Martín. In the north, it was Simón Bolívar. In Chile, it was Bernardo O'Higgins, the descendant of an Irish family that had settled in Spain generations earlier. All were criollos.

They all fought Spanish armies for more than a decade, winning some battles and losing others. San Martín ousted the Spaniards from Argentina and, in a stunning feat of military skill, led his army across the Andes in 1817 to help liberate Chile. In the north, Bolívar defeated the Spanish at the Battle of Boyacá in 1819, which marked the liberation of Colombia.

In Brazil, meanwhile, things were more peaceful. When Napoleon took over Portugal in 1808, Emperor João VI fled to Brazil. When he returned to Portugal in 1821, his son remained behind and declared Brazilian independence in 1821 without firing a shot.

That same year Lima, the seat of Spanish power, fell to the combined forces of San Martín and Bolívar. Spanish control was definitively ended when General Antonio José de Sucre defeated and captured Viceroy José de la Serna at the Battle of Ayacucho in 1824.

All of South America had become independent except for the Guianas, where Holland, France, and England held on to their colonies.

The Young Republics

The political map of South America in the years immediately after independence was different from what it is now. Present-day Colombia, Ecuador, and Venezuela made up a single nation called Gran Colombia. In the south, a government centered in Buenos Aires was so weak it barely had any influence on the provinces outside the city.

Civil wars as well as international wars redrew the map in the following decades. Argentina and Brazil fought each other to a standstill in a struggle that led to Uruguayan independence. Gran Colombia defeated Peru in a war, but then Venezuela and Ecuador seceded, leaving only Colombia behind. Bolivia invaded Peru, and the two nations formed a single nation for three years. Chile conquered Bolivia's coastline, leaving it landlocked. Chile also fought and defeated Peru. In the bloodiest war of all, nearly half the adult male population of Paraguay was killed in the War of the Triple Alliance against Argentina, Brazil, and Uruguay.

Shortly after becoming dictator of Paraguay in 1862, Francisco Solano López involved the country in the disastrous War of the Triple Alliance. By the time the war ended in 1870, Paraguay had lost more than half its population. It would take decades before the country recovered.

Wars weren't the only sources of hardship. Dictators rose to power nearly everywhere, and the economic gap between the criollo elite and blacks, Indians, and mestizos remained very wide.

Yet there were bright spots in Brazil and the Southern Cone. Brazilian coffee and rubber, Chilean copper, and Argentinean or Uruguayan beef and wheat boosted growing economics toward the end of the 19th century. Moderately stable, relatively democratic governments came to power, attracting millions of immigrants, mostly from Spain and Italy but also from Germany, eastern Europe, Ireland, and even rich and powerful Great Britain. The Europeans helped to shape the character of those nations, much like immigrants of similar origins shaped the United States.

South America Today

As the 20th century opened, South America presented a mixed picture. There were cities as sophisticated as any in Europe or North America. Yet there was widespread poverty, especially among people who were not white. And while nations of the Southern Cone experienced a period of democracy, dictators held sway nearly everywhere else.

The continent stayed on the fringes of world history. There was little South American involvement in either of the two world wars. But some South American leaders, most notably Getúlio Vargas in Brazil and Juan Domingo Perón in Argentina, were influenced by *fascism*. In other places, however, democracy made strides: the Venezuelans overthrew dictator Marcos Pérez Jiménez, while Uruguay and Chile further developed their long-standing democratic traditions.

The next global conflict was the *cold war*, and in that struggle South America was very directly affected. In the mid-1960s, left-wing guerrillas rose up in much of the continent, often finding military support from the *communist* regime of Fidel Castro. Castro's top aide, Argentinean Ernesto "Che" Guevara, was killed in Bolivia in 1967 while leading one of those uprisings.

Reaction to the revolts was harsh. In most countries, factions led by right-wing generals overthrew governments they considered too weak to stand up to the communist rebels. In Chile, socialist Salvador Allende was elected president in 1971, but he was later toppled in a *golpe de estado* by military leaders who claimed he was preparing to become a dictator. In his place, Augusto Pinochet ruled as a dictator.

By the 1970s, Guyana had gained independence from Great Britain and Suriname had broken away from Holland. Elsewhere in South America, the decade was a dark time. Democracy survived in Colombia and Venezuela, but the other Latin nations were ruled by dictators whose secret police squads were known to make citizens "disappear" without a trace. People caught in the crossfire between guerrillas and the military were kidnapped, jailed, tortured, and killed. Among the most vicious of the guerrilla groups was Peru's Sendero Luminoso, or "Shining Path."

However, international pressure and the defeat of most guerrilla groups caused the generals to turn over power to democratically elected governments in the 1980s. In Argentina, the change came about after military rulers lost a 1982 war against Great Britain for control of the Falklands, which Argentineans call the Malvinas and have claimed for nearly two centuries.

Today, the gap between the rich and the poor still looms wide. Corruption is rampant, and public discontent with government is high. For years, Colombia has been plagued by a civil war, a brutal and confusing struggle involving the Colombian army, drug dealers, the last major left-wing guerrilla army in South America, and gunmen in the pay of landowners threatened by the guerrillas. In Argentina, which was ranked among the world's dozen richest countries 100 years ago, the national economy nearly went bankrupt in late 2001. And in 2002, there was a failed *golpe* against Venezuelan president Hugo Chávez, a left-wing populist elected in 1998.

Yet, democracy is hanging on. In the early years of the 21st century, for the first time in South American history, the head of state of every government had been democratically elected.

(Opposite) Traders on the floor of Argentina's stock exchange in Buenos Aires. A financial crisis in 2000–2002 battered the country's economy. (Right) A fishing boat drifts past a petrochemical plant at Los Taques, Venezuela. Oil is Venezuela's most valuable resource; the country is one of the world's leading exporters of petroleum products.

3 The Economy

SOUTH AMERICA IS a middle-income region, not as wealthy as Western Europe and North America, not as poor as Africa and parts of Asia.

But there are different levels of economic well-being among the continent's nations. In 2000 the per capita income of Argentina was $12,900, about the same as that of the wealthiest nations of eastern Europe. Yet in Bolivia the per capita income was only $2,600, roughly equal to that of Zimbabwe and other African countries. Even *within* most nations, the gap between the rich and the poor is wider than it is nearly anywhere else in the world. In Peru, for instance, the poorest 10 percent of the people consume less than 2 percent of everything consumed in the nation, while the wealthiest 10 percent earn and consume more than one-third.

For most of the 20th century, governments either ignored the inequalities between the rich and poor or tried to foster growth through a more centralized economy. Inequalities persisted, and by the 1980s inflation had reached 200 percent in some countries—in other words, the price of almost everything people bought was doubling two times in one year.

Then, in the 1990s, after South Americans freed themselves of military dictatorial rule, most governments initiated *free market* reforms. But these reforms have not solved economic problems, either. Some people say the new democracies went too far in embracing *capitalism* and as their example cite Argentina, where the economy nearly collapsed in late 2001 after the government initiated *privatization* measures. Others say governments did not go far enough and point to Chile, where some believe privatization made the economy the fastest-growing of the continent.

Agriculture

Agriculture remains extremely important to South American economies, particularly the less developed ones. It makes up the largest part of the *gross domestic product (GDP)* in Guyana, for instance; in Ecuador, bananas and fresh-cut flowers alone account for nearly one-quarter of all export earnings.

Farming and ranching remain important among the more developed countries, too. Argentina and Uruguay are famous for their leather goods and high-quality beef. Brazil and Colombia produce large amounts of coffee. Chile not only makes world-class wines, but has also learned to take advantage of the reversal of seasons between the Northern and Southern

Hemisphere: it exports fresh fruits and vegetables to northern nations during their winter, which is summer in Chile.

Industry

Industry in South America is unevenly developed. It is almost non-existent in some of the poorer countries except as it relates to domestic agriculture or mining: Bolivia is a major processor of tin from its mines, and Paraguay is a major processor of oils from locally grown seeds.

Heavy manufacturing is concentrated in the Río de la Plata and Rio de Janeiro–São Paulo regions. Here are steel mills, motor vehicle plants, cement facto-

A Peruvian farmer sells his wares in a market in Cuzco.

ries, clothing factories, and shoemakers. Transport equipment and auto parts make up 16.6 percent of Brazilian exports, the largest single segment, with metallurgical products close behind at 10.7 percent. Other nations, including Colombia and Chile, also have industrial centers. A fairly new industry is the production of electricity through hydropower, dominated by Paraguay's huge Brazilian-built dams and power stations.

Mining

In some countries, mining and related activities are the most important part of the economy. Bolivia depends on tin exports, Peru's leading exports are gold and copper, and 70 percent of Suriname's export earnings come from sales of

Small boats navigate a thruway in the river town of Cartagena del Charia, in southern Colombia. This region has become one of the biggest producers of cocaine, and, rather than using Colombian money, many residents trade coca leaves and other materials used to make the drug for items they need.

bauxite. In Venezuela, which has for decades been among the world's top 10 oil producers, the petroleum sector accounts for nearly one-third of the GDP and around 80 percent of export earnings.

Services and the Black Market

The service sector is of increasing importance in South America, especially in regions with literate, better-trained populations, such as southern Brazil, Río de la Plata, and Chile. Because of its increased trade, Chile has developed strong sectors in export-import, banking, and other financial services.

Although there are no reliable figures, experts believe the underground economies of Paraguay and some of the Andean nations constitute a large but hidden and illegal part of the economy. In the Andean nations, the illegal economy has to do with cocaine trafficking. Coca leaf is grown mostly in Peru and Bolivia, and processed and sold largely in Colombia.

In Paraguay, illegal activities center on the unlicensed import of consumer goods such as television sets, stereos, perfume, and liquor, which are then sold on the black market in Argentina and Brazil.

Quick Facts: The Leading Products of South American Nations

Argentina

Agriculture: livestock, sunflower seeds, lemons, soybeans, grapes, corn, peanuts, tea, wheat.

Industry/Mining: food processing, motor vehicles, consumer goods, textiles and leather manufacturing, chemicals, steel.

Bolivia

Agriculture: soybeans, coffee, coca, cotton, corn, sugarcane, rice, potatoes, timber.

Industry/Mining: tin, zinc, silver, food and beverages, tóbacco, handicrafts, clothing.

Brazil

Agriculture: coffee, soybeans, wheat, rice, corn, sugarcane, cocoa, citrus, beef.

Industry/Mining: textiles, shoes, chemicals, cement, lumber, iron ore, steel, aircraft, motor vehicles, other machinery.

Chile

Agriculture: wheat, corn, grapes, beans, potatoes, fruit, livestock, wool, fish, timber.

Industry/Mining: copper, fish processing, iron and steel, wood products, transport equipment, cement, textiles.

Colombia

Agriculture: coffee, flowers, bananas, rice, tobacco, corn, sugarcane, cocoa beans, oilseed, vegetables.

Industry/Mining: textiles, food processing, footwear, beverages, chemicals, cement, gold, emeralds.

Ecuador

Agriculture: bananas, coffee, cocoa, rice, potatoes, manioc, sugarcane, cattle, sheep, pigs, fish, shrimp.

Industry/Mining: petroleum, food processing, textiles, paper and wood products, plastics, fishing.

Guyana

Agriculture: sugar, rice, wheat, vegetable oils, beef, pork, poultry, dairy products.
Industry/Mining: bauxite, sugarcane processing, rice milling, timber, fishing textiles, gold.

Paraguay

Agriculture: cotton, sugarcane, soybeans, corn, wheat, tobacco, fruits, vegetables, livestock, timber.
Industry/Mining: hydroelectric power production, oils, cement, textiles, beverages, wood products.

Peru

Agriculture: coffee, cotton, sugarcane, rice, wheat, potatoes, plantains, coca, livestock, dairy, wool, fish.
Industry/Mining: gold, copper, petroleum, textiles, food processing, cement, auto assembly, steel, shipbuilding.

Suriname

Agriculture: rice, bananas, palm kernels, coconuts, plantains, livestock, timber, shrimp.
Industry/Mining: bauxite and gold, alumina production, lumber, food processing, fish processing.

Uruguay

Agriculture: wheat, rice, barley, corn, sorghum, livestock, fish.
Industry/Mining: food processing, electrical machinery, transport equipment, textiles, chemicals, beverages.

Venezuela

Agriculture: corn, sorghum, sugarcane, rice, bananas, vegetables, coffee, beef, pork, milk, eggs, fish.
Industry/Mining: petroleum, iron ore, construction materials, food processing, textiles, steel, aluminum, motor vehicle assembly.

Source: CIA World Factbook, 2002.

(Opposite) Native children in the Amazon Basin of Peru. Amerindians make up just a small percentage of South America's more than 350 million people. (Right) A modern-day *gaucho*, or cowboy, on horseback in the Argentine Pampas.

4 The People

AS A GROUP OF nations on the same continent, South America is a geographical unit, but it is not a cultural unit. There is no such thing as a "South American culture" shared by the continent's 14 political subdivisions. Instead, there are several cultures, and the most striking cultural differences may be between the 10 Latin nations (Portuguese-speaking Brazil plus the 9 Spanish-speaking republics) and the rest of South America.

The Guianas

The people of Guyana, a former British colony, speak mostly English. A little less than half the population are descendants of immigrants from India, which was also once a British colony. The rest are black or *mulatto*—mixed

Quick Facts: The People of South America

Population: 350,822,240 (total)
Argentina: 37,812,817
Bolivia: 8,445,134
Brazil: 176,029,560
Chile: 15,498,930
Colombia: 41,008,227
Ecuador: 13,447,494
Falkland Islands: 2,967
French Guiana: 182,333
Guyana: 698,209
Paraguay: 5,884,491
Peru: 27,949,631
Suriname: 436,494
Uruguay: 3,386,575
Venezuela: 24,287,670

Religions: Mostly Catholic; evangelical Protestants gaining converts; large numbers of Jews in the Southern Cone; Hindus and Muslims in Guyana and Suriname.

Languages: Spanish, Portuguese, English, French, Dutch, Quechua, Aymara, Guaraní, plus as many as 1,000 other Indian languages and dialects.

Growth rate, 1990–2000: 1.82%
Projected growth rate, 2000–2025: 1.23% (2001 est.)

All figures are July 2002 estimates unless otherwise indicated.
Sources: CIA World Factbook, 2002; *Oxford Atlas of the World*, 2001.

white and black. Their culture more closely resembles the English-speaking Caribbean than it does the majority of Latin South America.

Suriname has a similar mixture of East Indians, blacks, and mixed-race people, but as a former Dutch colony its official language is Dutch, and much of the culture is Dutch-influenced.

French Guiana, still governed by France, has mostly blacks and mulattos, with East Indian and Chinese minorities. French is the common language.

Latin South America

Brazil and the Spanish-speaking nations of Argentina, Bolivia, Chile, Colombia, Ecuador, Paraguay, Peru, Uruguay, and Venezuela have enough in common to be grouped together as "Latin" South America. They inherited customs and traditions from their colonizers, Spain and Portugal—two neighbors on the *Iberian Peninsula* that have much in common themselves.

For instance, these nations all share certain forms of architecture, like whitewashed country homes with red-tiled roofs. They share a traditional form of Catholic worship too, emphasizing devotion to the Virgin Mary. And they share Latin traditions like the close family unit and the siesta—though the leisurely nap after lunch is disappearing under the pressures of modern life.

Yet there are differences among these Latin countries as well. The most noticeable differences are those between Brazil, with its Portuguese culture and language, and the nine countries whose culture and language is rooted at least partly in Spain. Even among the nine Spanish-speaking countries there are differences, which came about mainly because of the way different groups of people mixed—or failed to mix—throughout each country's history.

Brazil, the Continent's Giant

Brazil stands apart from its Latin cousins in South America because it is so big (almost as large as all other countries combined) and because of its Portuguese culture. Spanish-speakers can understand each other even in the different accents of Caracas and Buenos Aires, but generally they cannot understand Portuguese-speaking Brazilians. Brazilians, however, understand Spanish much more readily—a phenomenon attributed to the Spanish language's more straightforward pronunciation.

African culture is central to Brazil. Fifty-five percent of the population is white, mostly of Portuguese origin, but 45 percent is either black or mulatto.

Their influence can be seen in the *samba* music of Brazil, and also in the *candomblé* religious rituals, which combine Catholicism with traditional African tribal beliefs. The food, too, has both European and African influences. The national dish, *feijoada*, combines black beans with Portuguese sausages and pork.

Most Brazilians live in cities. Some live in magnificent homes, some in poverty-stricken neighborhoods called favelas. Throughout South America, Brazilians have a reputation for celebrating life. They are famous for their colorful carnivals, for the beaches at Rio de Janeiro, and for their love of soccer.

Drummers take part in a festive parade. South America has a rich culture, which has been influenced by the many groups of people who immigrated to the continent.

The Caribbean North

African traditions meld with Spanish traditions in Venezuela and coastal Colombia, which makes this region more similar to countries of the Spanish-speaking Caribbean, such as Cuba and Puerto Rico, than to its continental neighbors. For instance, the most popular sport in Venezuela is baseball, not soccer as in most South American countries.

The best-known cultural products are music and literature. Colombia has the *cumbia* style of music; Venezuela has various styles played with guitars. In both countries, African rhythms blend with Spanish melodies. Among the best-known writers from the region is the Colombian Gabriel García Márquez, winner of the Nobel Prize in literature in 1982.

Away from the coasts, deep in the tropical forest, Indian tribes have kept themselves apart from the Afro-Hispanic culture that dominates the region.

The Andes

This region includes Bolivia, Peru, Ecuador, and some inland parts of Colombia. Before the arrival of the Spanish, this was the home of highly developed Indian cultures, the most advanced of which were the Incas. Most residents are mestizo, but a large percentage is of Indian origin.

Indian cultures continue to influence life here. Traditional woven cloths and pottery are still made in the old pre-Columbian style. Music combines Spanish guitars with ancient Andean flutes. Food is based primarily around a type of potato that is original to the Andes.

Bolivia has the strongest Amerindian culture. More than half the people are Quechua or Aymara, and many speak those languages in their homes, speaking Spanish only in public. The population of Peru is 45 percent Indian, and it is here that the most magnificent Inca ruins can be found, including the lost city of Machu Picchu. Ecuador is about 25 percent Indian. Colombia has few Indians, and except for isolated Amazon tribes, everyone speaks Spanish. Fifty-eight percent of Colombians are mestizo.

The Southern Cone

The most European region of South America is its narrow southern section, composed of Argentina, Chile, Paraguay, and Uruguay. There was little African slavery here during colonial times, so African culture has had minimal influence. Likewise, there were no advanced Indian civilizations, so Indian influence is also minimal. An exception to the rule is Paraguay, where the culture of the Guaraní Indians is an important part of the national identity. Most Paraguayans are bilingual in Spanish and Guaraní. Yet even in Paraguay, most people are mestizo and there are few pure-blooded Indians.

Argentina, Chile, and Uruguay are more-typical Southern Cone nations, with mostly white populations. Many inhabitants are of Spanish origin, but perhaps an equal number descend from other Europeans—in the 19th century millions of Italians, Germans, Irish, Britons, and eastern European Jews immigrated not just to the United States, but also to the Southern Cone.

Those immigrants today have become part of the mainstream cultures, helping make each of their countries a South American melting pot. The European influences are still prominent. In Argentina, for instance, pasta is one of the more popular foods, and Italian surnames are as common as

The Spanish influence on South America, particularly in the countries of the Southern Cone region, can be seen in the culture today. Spanish sports such as bull-fighting remain popular in many South American countries.

Spanish surnames. The local accent, too, makes Spanish sound like Italian.

The region produced some of the world's leading writers of the 20th century. They include Argentineans Jorge Luis Borges and Julio Cortázar and Chilean poets Pablo Neruda and Gabriela Mistral, both winners of the Nobel Prize in literature.

Off the coast of Argentina, in the windswept South Atlantic, is the British dependency of the Falkland Islands. Most residents are shepherds or fishermen of British descent, and the official language is English. They see themselves as overseas Britons.

(Opposite) The statue of Christ the Redeemer looks over the harbor at Rio de Janeiro, Brazil. The statue atop Corcovado Mountain is 125 feet (38 meters) tall. (Right) A busy street in Buenos Aires, Argentina. With 13 million inhabitants, Buenos Aires is the largest city in South America and one of the largest in the world.

5 The Cities

Argentina

By far the largest city is the sophisticated capital, Buenos Aires, with its broad boulevards and European-style cafés. It is the most populous on the continent, with nearly 13 million people. Córdoba, the next largest city, has 1.5 million inhabitants.

Bolivia

La Paz, population 811,400, is the world's highest capital, at an elevation of 12,000 feet (3,660 meters). The city retains a colonial atmosphere; its open-air markets are crowded with merchants and customers in traditional Andean Indian garb. The largest city is Santa Cruz, with 1.1 million residents.

Brazil

Brazil has 13 cities of more than 1 million people, with three other cities approaching that number. The largest, São Paulo, has 10 million residents and is considered the country's economic center and business engine; its *metropolitan* area of 18.5 million is the most heavily populated in South America. About 220 miles (354 km) away is Rio de Janeiro, population 6 million, with its famous Copacabana and Ipanema beaches and spectacular Sugar Loaf Mountain on Guanabara Bay. Brazil's capital, Brasília, has 2 million people; it was built in the 1950s and 1960s as an expression of ultra-modern architecture.

Chile

Santiago's 5 million people make it the home of nearly one-third of Chileans. The Plaza de Armas dates from 1541, but there are also skyscrapers with businesses that support South America's strongest economy. Charming seaside Viña del Mar, population 359,000, hosts an annual music festival that attracts pop stars from throughout the Spanish-speaking world.

Colombia

With 6.7 million people, the capital of Bogotá has a high crime rate and bands of homeless children roaming the streets, but also cultured, sophisti-cated residents with a reputation as intellectuals and lovers of literature who pride themselves on speaking the best Spanish in South America. Other large cities are Cali, population 2.2 million, and Medellín, 1.8 million.

A view of crowded Quito, capital of Ecuador.

Ecuador

Guayaquil, population 2.2 million, and Quito, population 1.6 million, have long carried on a rivalry. Quito, the capital, is a colonial mountain city whose residents have a reputation for sticking with traditions and restraining their emotions. Residents of Guayaquil, on the Pacific coast lowlands, see themselves as modern and lively.

Falkland Islands

The capital of Port Stanley, with 1,800 people, is the only population center in these barren, lonely islands. The rest of the Falklanders, only about 500 more people, live in the countryside.

French Guiana

Only about 60,000 people live in sleepy Cayenne, the capital of this sparsely populated overseas province of France.

Guyana

Georgetown, population 164,000, is the capital and only city with more than 50,000 inhabitants. St. George's Anglican Cathedral is said to be the world's largest wooden building.

Paraguay

The capital of Asunción has only 547,000 inhabitants within its city limits, but the metropolitan area is home to more than twice that many. It has a relatively quiet atmosphere. Ciudad del Este, near the giant Itaipú hydro-electric plant, is the only other large town or city outside metropolitan Asunción. It has grown to 285,000 inhabitants since its founding in 1957.

Peru

No city on the continent has a more impressive colonial center than Lima, population 7.6 million. From its Plaza Mayor, viceroys ruled the Spanish Empire in South America for nearly 300 years. Far from coastal Lima, in the Andean highlands, is the ancient Inca capital of Cuzco. It is only the ninth-largest city in Peru, but its architecture makes it a huge outdoor museum.

Suriname

The capital of Suriname, and its largest city, is Paramaribo, which has a population of about 200,000. The city is located on the west bank of the Suriname River. A number of buildings in Paramaribo date back to the first half of the 18th century; they were built during the Dutch colonial period. Other important cities in Suriname are Lelydorp (population 17,000) and Nieuw Nickerie (population 13,000).

Uruguay

Few other world capitals dominate their nations as much as Montevideo, whose population of 1.8 million constitutes more than half of Uruguay's total. It is a major port on the Río de la Plata, with broad avenues and *ornate* architecture. Montevideo is also famous for its beaches and elegant hotels, a tourist destination for rich Argentineans and European nobility.

Venezuela

Colonial buildings stand next to sleek skyscrapers in the capital of Caracas, population 1.7 million. This once sleepy city was transformed by money from Venezuela's petroleum earnings beginning in the 1930s. It remains the nation's financial hub, but the center of the oil industry is Maracaibo, whose population is actually larger by about 300,000.

A Calendar of South American Festivals

January

Every South American nation celebrates **New Year's Day**. January 6 is **Epiphany**, a holiday that tradition holds marks the day when the Three Wise Men visited the baby Jesus bearing gifts. To celebrate the day, South American parents give their children gifts.

February

Venezuela celebrates the **Feast of the Virgin of Candelaria** on February 2. February 23 is Guyana's **Republic Day**. And late February to mid-March, just before the Catholic fasting period of **Lent**, is **Carnival** season throughout South America. Most countries have different versions of the Carnival festivity, the most famous of them taking place in Rio de Janeiro.

March

Catholics in Latin nations observe **St. Joseph's Day** on March 19. Suriname and Guyana, with their large Asian and Indian populations, celebrate **Phagwa**, the Hindu New Year, early in the month.

April

On April 21, the Falklands celebrate **Queen Elizabeth's Birthday** in honor of their British monarch. On the same day, Brazilians hold **Tiradentes Day** to mark the execution in 1792 of Joaquim José da Silva Xavier, also known as Tiradentes (Tooth-puller), who led an uprising against the Portuguese colonists.

May

Most nations hold **May Day** ceremonies on May 1 to honor working people. On May 10, Argentina marks the **Revolution of 1810**. May 15 is **Paraguayan Independence Day**. On May 21, Chileans remember the defeat of the Peruvian navy at the **Battle of Iquique** in 1879, and on the 24th, Ecuador commemorates the **Battle of Pichincha** during the struggle for independence.

June

On June 10, **Malvinas Day**, Argentineans affirm their claim of sovereignty over the British-held Malvinas, or Falkland Islands. On the 14th, Falklanders celebrate **Liberation Day**, the defeat of Argentine forces during their invasion in 1982. June 12 is **Peace of Chaco Day** in Paraguay, the anniversary of the end of the victorious war over Bolivia in 1935. June 19 in Uruguay is the **Birthday of José Artigas**, the father of the nation. And on June 29, most of the Latin nations celebrate **St. Peter and St. Paul Day**.

July

July is full of patriotic holidays in South America. Four nations mark **Independence Day** this month: Venezuela on the 5th, Argentina on the 9th, Colombia on the 20th, and Peru on the 28th. French Guiana celebrates **Bastille Day** on July 14, the anniversary of the symbolic start of the French Revolution in 1789. In addition, Uruguay has **Constitution Day** on the 18th, while Bolivia, Colombia, Ecuador, and Venezuela mark the

A Calendar of South American Festivals

Birthday of Simón Bolívar, the Liberator, on July 24. Festivities continue in Ecuador the following day to mark the **Founding of Guayaquil**.

August

This month brings more patriotic celebrations. There are three **Independence Days**: August 6 in Bolivia, August 10 in Ecuador, and August 25 in Uruguay. In addition, Colombians celebrate victory in the **Battle of Boyacá** during the War of Independence on August 7, and Argentineans observe the **Death of José de San Martín**, the nation's founding father, on August 17. Most nations celebrate August 15 as the Catholic feast of the Virgin Mary's **Assumption**, especially Paraguay, where it is also the anniversary of the **Founding of Asunción**, the capital city. One day later Paraguay observes the **Day of the Child**, when schools are closed to honor the child soldiers who died in battle at the end of the War of the Triple Alliance.

September

September brings **Independence Day** for Brazil on the 7th and Chile on the 18th. On the 29th, Paraguayans celebrate their country's victory over Bolivia during the **Battle of Boquerón**.

October

October 8 in Peru is the anniversary of the **Battle of Angamos** during the Pacific War against Chile. On October 12, Brazilians observe the **Feast of Our Lady of Aparecida**, the country's patron

saint. And on the same day, despite protests from Indian groups, the Spanish-speaking countries celebrate their common heritage from Spain in **Día de La Raza**, the anniversary of Columbus's arrival in the Americas.

November

Many South Americans continue the tradition of visiting the graves of their deceased family members on November 1–2, **All Souls' Day**. On November 11, the anniversary of the armistice ending World War I, French Guiana follows the custom of its mother country in holding **Veterans' Day** ceremonies. November 25 is **Independence Day** in Suriname. Also in Suriname, as well as in Guyana, Hindus observe **Divali**, the religious Festival of Lights.

December

Ecuadorians celebrate the **Founding of Quito** on December 6. On the 8th, Brazil and the Spanish-speaking nations observe the Catholic **Feast of the Immaculate Conception**, which begins the **Christmas** season. Christmas, of course, is observed in every South American nation. It includes not only Christmas Day but also Christmas Eve, when many families traditionally have their holiday meal.

Recipes

Argentinean *Chimichurri* Sauce

There are as many different versions as there are Argentineans, but everyone uses chimichurri as the accompaniment for a traditional parrillada, a barbecue with the country's world-famous beef.

1 cup olive oil
1 bunch fresh parsley
Juice of one fresh lemon
4 cloves of garlic
1 tsp fresh oregano
Salt and pepper to taste

Directions:
1. Blend all the ingredients in a food processor.
2. Pour the mix onto the steaks, reserving some for later.
3. Refrigerate the reserved *chimichurri* in a separate container from the marinated steaks for 4–6 hours.
4. Grill the steaks while basting with the marinade liquid but not the reserve, which can be slightly heated and spooned over the beef when ready to serve.

Brazilian *Feijoada*

The national dish of Brazil is this hearty beef and bean soup combining European and African influences.

8 cups dried black beans
3 lbs *carne seca* (Brazilian salted cured beef), cut into 1" pieces
2 lbs Portuguese *chouriço* or other sweet sausage, cut into 1" pieces
2 lbs baby back spareribs, sliced into two-rib sections
2 bay leaves
1 large onion, chopped
2 cloves garlic, minced
3 tbsp olive oil

Directions:
1. Soak the beans overnight with water to cover at least 3–4". Soak the *carne seca* in water also.
2. The next morning, drain the beans and place in a large pot with water to cover by at least 3".
3. Bring the beans to a boil in medium heat and add the meats. Simmer for two hours or until soft, stirring from time to time and adding water as necessary to keep beans covered.
4. Heat the olive oil in a skillet and toss in the onion and garlic, sautéing until golden brown, then add to simmering beans.
5. Take two spoonfuls of beans, mash them, and put them back into the pot to thicken. Add bay leaves and continue to simmer at least another hour, adding water as necessary.

Colombian *Patacones* (Fried Green Plantain)

Green plantains are easy to make, and delicious as a side dish, like french fries.

1. Peel the plantains and slice in round pieces about 1" wide. Fry in hot oil until color begins to turn gold.
2. Take out of oil, cover with wax paper or a brown paper bag, and pound flat, about 1/2" thick, with a kitchen mallet or a heavy can.
3. Return to hot oil and cook until golden and soft.

Bolivian *Sopa de Maní* (Peanut Soup)

10 cups beef broth
1/2 cup raw peanuts, shelled and ground in the blender
1/4 cup rice
1 tbsp yellow chili powder
Salt to taste
5 potatoes, cut julienne style and fried until golden crisp
Chopped fresh parsley for garnish

Directions:
1. Boil all ingredients except the potatoes and simmer for half an hour.
2. Add fried potatoes plus the parsley and serve.

Venezuelan Corn Pancakes *(Cachapas)*

3 cups frozen corn kernels (canned corn may be used)
1 tsp baking soda
1/2 to 3/4 cup milk (depending on how tender the corn is)
1/2 cup sugar
1 egg
1/2 cup regular flour
1/2 cup cornmeal

Directions:
1. Combine all the ingredients in a blender or food processor. The mix should become thick. If not, add some cornmeal.
2. Pour the mix into small pancakes approximately 1/2" thick and about 5" across on a hot skillet coated with oil or nonstick spray. Let the pancakes cook on medium heat for about one minute on each side, or until small bubbles form on the top.
3. Cachapas should be served hot, but they can be reheated in a microwave for 30 seconds. Put shredded white cheese, butter, or jelly on them.

Glossary

Antarctica—the southernmost continent, including the South Pole.

autonomous—self-governing.

biodiversity—an abundance of many kinds of living things.

canopy—in a forest, the uppermost layer formed by branches of trees.

capitalism—an economic system under which goods and services are produced by private enterprise, with little participation from the government.

cold war—the period of rivalry between the United States and the Soviet Union, from 1945 to 1991, during which there was little open fighting but much political and economic conflict.

communist— relating to an authoritarian economic system called communism, under which goods and services are produced by the government, with no private enterprise permitted.

coniferous—trees that do not shed their leaves in winter, such as pine trees.

criollos—people born in Latin America; in past centuries, the term referred more specifically to the descendants of white European settlers.

deciduous—trees that shed their leaves in winter, like oaks and maples.

deforestation—the cutting down of forests for lumber or to clear land for farming.

ecosystem—the community of plants and animals along with their natural environment.

endemic—said of a species that exists only in a particular area.

fascism—an authoritarian political system that glorifies national and racial groups above individuals.

fjords—a Norwegian word that refers to narrow sea inlets bounded by cliffs.

free market—an economic system that operates by open competition; part of capitalism.

golpe de estado—a Spanish term referring to a violent change of government; a coup d'etat.

glaciers—large bodies of ice and snow that slowly spread over a land area.

gross domestic product (GDP)—the total value of goods and services produced by a nation annually.

hierarchy—a classification or ranking of people according to their social or economic standing.

Iberian Peninsula—the part of western Europe where Spain and Portugal are located.

mestizo—a person of mixed European and Indian ancestry.

metropolitan—relating to the region including a major city and surrounding suburbs or towns.

mulatto—a person of mixed European and black African blood.

nomadic—a term describing a culture that roams from place to place, without a settled home.

ornate—elaborately decorated.

privatization—the selling of government-owned companies to private firms.

Southern Cone—the narrow region in the lower third of South America.

tableland—a large plain at high altitude.

tropic of Capricorn—an imaginary line around the globe (at about the latitude 23.5°S) to mark the place where the sun is directly overhead when it reaches its southernmost point.

ursine—relating to members of the bear family.

Project and Report Ideas

Changing Borders

Make a map of modern South America showing the boundaries of each country. Make another map, showing the boundaries as they existed right after independence, in 1824. Write a report explaining how the frontiers changed, and why the changes are important.

South American Geography Map

Make a map of South America. Draw in the major regions outlined in the "Geography" section: Andes, Amazon Basin, Guiana Highlands, Orinoco Basin, Río de la Plata complex, Brazilian plateau, Pampas, Patagonia, Llanos, Pantanal, West Coast flatlands, Southern Chile coast. Color each area a different color.

South American Economic Map

Make a map of South America, showing each country. Label the two leading exports for each, and draw pictures to match. For instance, draw an oil well for Venezuela's petroleum, or the head of a cow for Uruguay's cattle industry.

Music

Listen to Andean flute music, an Argentinean tango, a Brazilian samba, and a Colombian cumbia. Write a paragraph for each, explaining how they sound to you and what instruments are used.

South American Animals

Get seven pieces of blank paper. On each one, write the name of 2 of the 14 South American political units (put one name at the top and another in the middle of the page). Then find pictures of two mammals and two birds from each one. Write three to four sentences describing each one and its habitat.

Inca Writing

Find a photograph of a quipu, the knotted cotton cords of different lengths and colors with which Incas kept records. Using thick woolen yarn, try to imitate the pattern.

The Countries of South America: Maps

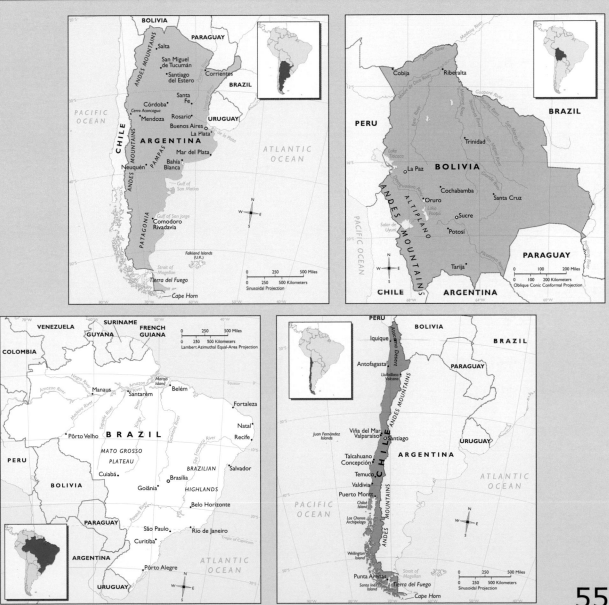

The Countries of South America: Maps

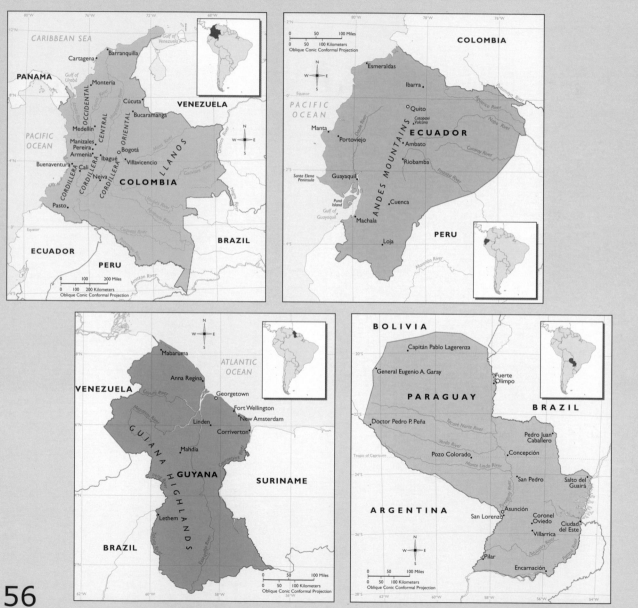

The Countries of South America: Maps

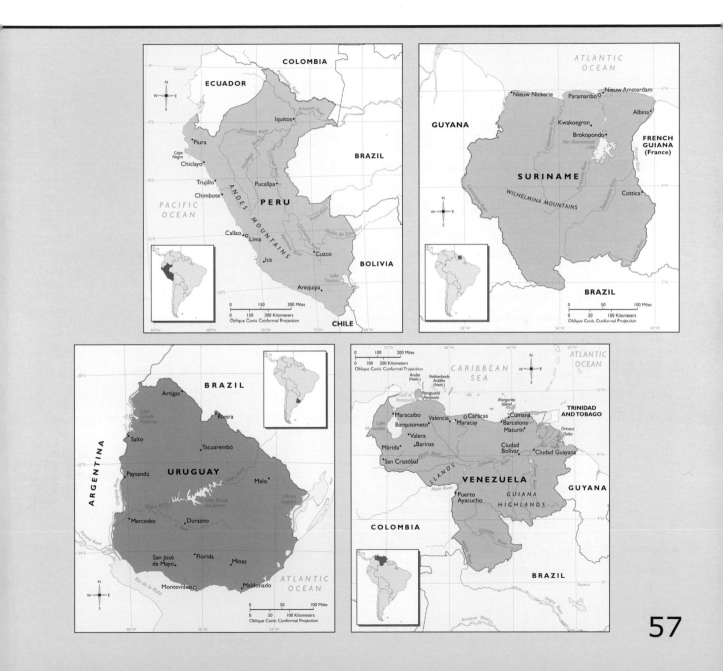

Chronology

Ca. 10,500 B.C. Human beings were living in a settlement in Monte Verde, Chile.

7000–4500 B.C. Ancient peoples leave evidence of settled farming communities near the Andes Mountains.

2000s B.C. Ancient people build first large ceremonial structures, in Peru.

900–200 B.C. The Chavín tribes settle along the Andes.

circa 200 B.C. Nazca culture develops in southern Peru.

A.D. 300–950 Tiahuanaco civilization flourishes near Lake Titicaca.

1200s The Inca Empire is born.

1498 Europeans first land on South American continent during Christopher Columbus's third voyage.

1500 Pedro Álvares Cabral claims Brazil for Portugal.

1532 Francisco Pizarro conquers Inca Empire for Spain.

1610–1767 Jesuits establish missions in Paraguay.

1776 The establishment of the Viceroyalty of Río de la Plata divides Spanish South America.

1810 With Spain and Portugal under Napoleonic control, criollos take over local governments; Portuguese emperor rules from exile in Brazil.

1811 Venezuela and Paraguay declare independence from Spain.

1816 Argentina declares independence, but remains a loose confederation of provinces.

1818 Chile declares independence.

1819 Colombia and Venezuela declare independence and form federation with Ecuador called the Gran Colombia.

1822 King Pedro declares Brazil independent from Portugal.

1824 General Antonio José de Sucre's victory at Ayacucho expels the last Spanish forces; Peru gains independence.

1825 Bolivia declares independence; Uruguayan patriots gain independence from Brazil.

1830 Republic of Gran Colombia breaks up; dictators rule nearly everywhere.

1864–70 Paraguay fights disastrous War of the Triple Alliance against Brazil, Argentina, and Uruguay.

1862 Bartolomé Mitre becomes the first president of a united Argentina.

Chronology

1879–84	Chile defeats Peru and Bolivia in War of the Pacific.
1889	Pedro II abdicates from throne in Brazil and the country is proclaimed a republic.
1930	Getúlio Vargas becomes provisional president of Brazil; will rule as dictator 1937–45.
1932–35	Paraguay defeats Bolivia in Chaco War.
1946–55	Juan Domingo Perón holds power in Argentina.
1954	General Alfredo Stroessner takes power in Paraguay.
1960s–70s	Left-wing guerrillas unite and fight for control; in response, the military establishes power in all Latin countries but Colombia and Venezuela. Tens of thousands die during combat or are executed by right-wing "death squads."
1970	Salvador Allende is elected president in Chile, becoming the first Communist freely voted into power.
1973	Allende is overthrown; the military dictatorship of General Augusto Pinochet begins.
1982	Great Britain crushes Argentina's attempt to take the Malvinas/Falkland Islands.
1983	The election of Raúl Alfonsín ends military rule in Argentina.
1985	The election of Tancredo Neves ends military rule in Brazil.
1989	General Stroessner is ousted from power in Paraguay and Patricio Aylwin is elected president in Chile, ending the two countries' military dictatorships.
1990	Alberto Fujimori becomes president in Peru; begins successful fight against guerrilla group Sendero Luminoso.
1990s	Tens of thousands are killed in Colombian civil war; elsewhere, there is slow economic growth.
1998	Venezuelan president Hugo Chávez, sympathetic to socialism, steers country away from current privatization trends.
2001	In February, Colombian president Andrés Pastrana and rebel leader Manuel Marulanda Vélez sign a peace agreement at Los Pozos in an attempt to end civil war; in December, Argentinean citizens frustrated with poor economic conditions incite riots in Buenos Aires.
2002	A *golpe de estado* in Venezuela fails to remove left-wing populist leader Hugo Chávez; the Brazilian national soccer team wins the World Cup championship in June.

Further Reading/Internet Resources

Bethell, Leslie, ed. *A Cultural History of Latin America: Literature, Music and the Visual Arts in the 19th and 20th Centuries*. New York: Cambridge University Press, 1998.

Fuentes, Carlos. *The Buried Mirror: Reflections on Spain and the New World*. Boston: Houghton Mifflin, 1999.

Guillermoprieto, Alma. *Looking for History: Dispatches from Latin America*. New York: Vintage Books, 2002.

Lutz, Richard L. *Hidden Amazon: The Greatest Voyage in Natural History*. Salem, Oregon: DIMI Press, 1998.

Minnis, Natalie. *Insight Guide South America*. London, England: Insight Guides, 2002.

Mullin, Penn. *Postcards from South America*. Novato, Calif.: Academic Therapy, 1995.

Wood, Michael. *Conquistadors*. Berkeley, Calif.: University of California Press, 2001

History and Geography

http://www.jungletrekker.com
http://www.oas.org/children/menu1.html
http://www.msstate.edu/Archives/History/text/latext.html
http://www.worldhistorycompass.com/latin.htm
http://www.ibiblio.org/expo/1492.exhibit/Intro.html

Economic and Political Information

http://www.hrw.org/americas/index.php
http://www.lanic.utexas.edu/
http://qesdb.cdie.org/lac/index.html
http://www.zonalatina.com/

Culture and Festivals

http://gosouthamerica.about.com/library/weekly/aa011500a.htm
http://gosouthamerica.about.com/library/weekly/aa032702a.htm
http://otto.cmr.fsu.edu/~cma/
http://www.universes-in-universe.de//america/e_kont.htm
http://www.uky.edu/Subject/latinamlit.html
http://www.bbc.co.uk/worldservice/arts/features/latinamericanwords/index.shtml

Institute of the Americas
10111 North Torrey Pines Rd.
La Jolla, CA 92037
(858) 453-5560
http://ioa.ucsd.edu/defaultnet.html

Inter-American Defense Board
2600 16th St., N.W.
Washington, DC 20441
(202) 939-7490
http://www.jid.org/

Organization of American States
17th Street & Constitution Ave., N.W.
Washington, DC 20006
(202)458-3000
http://www.oas.org/

Pan American Health Organization
525 23d St., N.W.
Washington, DC 20037
(202) 974-3000
http://www.paho.org/

Rainforest Alliance
65 Bleecker St.
New York, NY 10012
(212) 677-1900
http://www.rainforest-alliance.org/

Summit of the Americas Center
Latin American and Caribbean Center
Florida International University
University Park, Miami, Florida 33199
(305) 348-2894
http://www.americasnet.net/SOAC_Home/
index.htm

Index

Allende, Salvador, 24
Africa, 20, 27, 37, 38, 39, 40
Amazon River, 10, 11, 12, 14–15
Andes Mountains, 9–10, 11, 12, 15,
    17–18, 21, 29–30, 31, 47
Angel Falls, 10
Antarctica, 9
Argentina, 10, 21, 22, 23, 24, 25, 27,
    28, 31, 36, 40–41, 43
Asunción, 46
Atacama Desert, 12
Atahuallpa, emperor of the Incas, 19
Atlantic Ocean, 10, 11, 15
Aymara language, 40

Bogotá, 12, 44
Bolívar, Simón, 21
Bolivia, 10, 18, 22, 24, 27, 29, 30, 31,
    36, 39–40, 43
Borges, Jorge Luis, 41
Boyacá, Battle of, 21
Brasília, 44
Brazil, 10, 12, 21, 22, 23, 28, 31, 35,
    36, 37, 43
Buenos Aires, 11, 20, 22, 37, 43

Cabral, Pedro Álvares, 20
Cali, 44
Cape Horn, 9
Caracas, 11, 20, 37, 47
Castro, Fidel, 24
Cayenne, 46
Charles V, king of Spain, 19
Chávez, Hugo, 25
Chavín Indians, 18
Chile, 9, 11, 12, 15, 18, 21, 22, 23, 24,
    28–29, 30, 31, 36, 40–41, 44

Ciudad del Este, 46
Colombia, 9, 18, 22, 24, 25, 28, 30, 31,
    36, 39–40, 44
Columbus, Christopher, 18
Córdoba, 43
Cortázar, Julio, 41
Cuba, 24, 39
Cuzco, 18, 46

Ecuador, 18, 22, 28, 36, 39–40, 45

Falkland Islands (Malvinas), 24, 41,
    45
France, 20, 21, 36
French Guiana, 46

García Márquez, Gabriel, 39
Georgetown, 46
Gran Colombia, 22
Great Britain (England), 20, 21, 23,
    24, 35, 41
Guaraní Indians, 40
Guayaquil, 45
Guevara, Ernesto "Che," 24
Guiana Highlands, 10, 11
Guyana, 24, 28, 35, 46

Inca Indians, 18, 19, 39

Jiménez, Marcos Pérez, 23
João VI, emperor of Portugal, 21

La Guajira Peninsula, 9
La Paz, 43
Lago de Maracaibo, 10
Lake Titicaca, 10
Lelydorp, 47

Lima, 20, 21, 46
Losada, Diego de, 20

Machu Picchu, 18, 40
Mendoza, Pedro de, 20
Mistral, Gabriela, 41
Medellín, 44
Montevideo, 47

Napoleon, 21
Nazca Indians, 18
Neruda, Pablo, 41
Netherlands, 20, 21, 24, 36
Nieuw Nickerie, 47

O'Higgins, Bernardo, 21
Orinoco River, 10, 11, 12, 15

Pacific Ocean, 11, 18
Pampas, 11, 15
Pantanal, 11
Paraguay, 22, 29, 30, 31, 36, 40–41, 46
Paraguay River, 10
Paramaribo, 47
Paraná River, 10
Patagonia, 11, 15
Perón, Juan Domingo, 23
Peru, 10, 18, 22, 24, 27, 30, 31, 36,
    39–40, 46
Pinochet, Augusto, 24
Pizarro, Francisco, 19
Port Stanley, 45
Portugal, 18, 20, 21, 37
Puerto Rico, 39

Quechua language, 18, 40
Quito, 45

Index/Picture Credits

Rio de Janeiro, 11, 29, 38, 44
Río de la Plata, 10, 29, 31, 47
Roman Catholic Church, 37, 38

San Martín, José de, 21
Santiago de Chile, 11, 44
São Francisco River, 10
São Paulo, 29, 44
Sendero Luminoso (Shining Path), 24
Serna, José de la, 21

South America
    economy of, 23, 27–33
    geography and climate of, 9–15
    history of, 17–25
    people and culture of, 35–41
    See also individual countries
Spain, 18, 19, 20, 21, 23, 37, 39
Sucre, Antonio José de, 21
Suriname, 24, 30, 36, 47
Suriname River, 47

Tiahuanaco Indians, 18

Tierra del Fuego, 12
Treaty of Tordesillas, 18

United States, 23
Uruguay, 10, 22, 23, 28, 36, 40–41, 47
Uruguay River, 10

Valdivia, Pedro de, 20
Vargas, Getúlio, 23
Venezuela, 10, 11, 22, 23, 24, 25, 30, 36, 39, 47
Viña del Mar, 44

Contributors

Senior Consulting Editor **James D. Henderson** is professor of international studies at Coastal Carolina University. He is the author of *Conservative Thought in Twentieth Century Latin America: The Ideals of Laureano Gómez* (1988; Spanish edition *Las ideas de Laureano Gómez* published in 1985); *When Colombia Bled: A History of the Violence in Tolima* (1985; Spanish edition *Cuando Colombia se desangró, una historia de la Violencia en metrópoli y provincia*, 1984); and coauthor of *A Reference Guide to Latin American History* (2000) and *Ten Notable Women of Latin America* (1978).

Mr. Henderson earned a bachelor's degree in history from Centenary College of Louisiana, and a master's degree in history from the University of Arizona. He then spent three years in the Peace Corps, serving in Colombia, before earning his doctorate in Latin American history in 1972 at Texas Christian University.

Roger E. Hernández writes a syndicated column distributed by King Features to some 40 newspapers across the country. He is coauthor of *Cubans in America*, an illustrated history of the Cuban presence in the United States. He also wrote a book on Paraguay for the DISCOVERING SOUTH AMERICA series. He teaches writing and journalism at the New Jersey Institute of Technology and Rutgers University.